THE DEFINITION OF
MELANCHOLY

POEMS

CLIFF BURNS

Cover design: Chris Kent
Cover photograph: Robert Postma
Interior Layout: Megan McCullough

Published by Black Dog Press (blackdogpress@yahoo.ca)

Printed by Lightning Source

ISBN: 978-1-7781520-0-9 (Print)
       978-1-7781520-1-6 (Ebook)

Also by Cliff Burns:

BLACK DOG PRESS

"Poetry can repair no loss, but defies the space which separates. And it does this by its continued labor of reassembling what has been scattered."

John Berger

"Poetry is a torture machine of language."

Slavoj Zizek

For Sherron

"When you are old and grey and full of sleep,
And nodding by the fire, take down this book,
And slowly read, and dream of the soft look
Your eyes had once, and of their shadows deep..."

W.B. Yeats

THE DEFINITION OF
MELANCHOLY

Endangered

We were moonlight children
suspended in the tide
playful, mischievous
a phosphorescent sheen
illuminating flashing limbs
naked and unabashed
oblivious of the long shapes
congregating beneath us
drawn by our impertinent laughter

Full Disclosure

I am not W.B. Yeats
my voices are small
I would not presume
to speak for any race
can barely articulate
my own petty desires

No exalted themes
flawless symbolism
of towers and gyres
more like a belated
cry for help rendered
inaudible by traffic noise

I am not part of any
collective consciousness
but an outlier lurking
in the weeds avoiding
the glare of headlights
and what they can reveal

Hermetic (2018 C.E.)

Retreat to my desert cave
await the dry rasp
of approaching footsteps;

Perhaps the Devil again
to try my simple faith
or some bright seraph
arrayed in perfect Grace

Sangfroid

Let it fall:
someone will eventually pick up the pieces
apply adhesive
arrange the fragments
into something resembling hope.

For Immediate Release

I am an Artist again
looking out through alien eyes
detached from worldly concerns
immersed in otherness

Resorting to obscure tongues
oblivious of their incomprehension
consciously frustrating expectations
the way they cling to forlorn hope

Self Help

I am unlearning the harm you've done,
teaching myself to forgive.

Your lessons, harshly enacted,
frequently employing corporal punishment.

Abuse under the guise of discipline,
shaming in the name of love.

If you'd just *once* stayed your hand
or bit that terrible tongue.

Pleading exhaustion and overwork
for the times you failed us.

The passage of years refuting
the healing powers of Time.

The way you evince innocence
while pretending you don't remember.

Toothless now, like an old lioness,
domesticated, deemed safe to approach.

If only they knew you in halcyon days,
when you were fearsome and killed for sport.

Gedankenexperiment

One must keep an open mind
in case something falls in
some errant idea
that caroms off another
reinventing the wheel
in a new and exciting way.

Einstein called them
"thought experiments"
and over the course
of one fateful day
imagined an ordered,
rational universe.

Similarly, *you* might
be inspired to conceive
of a society without sin
or rancor, be a herald
of great and wonderful tidings
a savior or, at least, a saint.

Shopping at Airports

I buy you at the Duty Free shop
assemble you when I get home.

Some hesitation before naming you,
though the warrantee terms are clear.

Still second-guessing my commitment
even as you open your eyes.

Lost Art

After Otto Dix we know
why they send them home
in closed caskets

The war dead lack elegance
refusing to conform to
classic depictions of beauty

Their wounds gape
wet and labial, inviting
unwelcome comparisons

Death and Eros
indecently clutching, an
untitled lost *gouache* on cardboard

The Reaping

We have *all* been damaged
to the extent that at some
point in our lives our defenses
have been breached leaving us
vulnerable to different
shades of abuse neglect
or outright violence.

Every single one of us has
endured ridicule and humiliation
at the hands of others.

And so none should plead special
circumstances or demand a lofty
place on the hierarchy of suffering
only (but not merely) an acknowledgement
of our secret ordeal.

We were gardeners (once) and should know that
from the smallest beginnings tall things grow.

Mind, then, where you scatter your thirsty seeds.

The Gardener

Hand-watering
doting on my favorites
an arbitrary god
drawn to bright colors

Homegrown Terror

People slinking down back alleys
    must have something to hide
subversives, if not terrorists
    avoiding prying eyes

They *seem* poor and tired
    but that could be just a front
they're probably a sleeper cell
    dreaming of martyrdom

The Bear

The last mild day
before the long night

Feeling the tug of wintersleep
shivering under snowy blankets

By December pining
for the drip of meltwater

Ensconced in my stuffy den
squirming with restless cubs

Ancestor Worship

hold on
help is coming
from the future
a reaching hand
defying Fate

2:00 p.m. (at the Broadway Roastery)

People-watching as I drink green tea
my window on the world clear, the view
unobstructed, my presence invisible to
the men and women rushing by, harried,
anxious, even the street characters
looking grim behind their patchy
beards and multiple layers of clothing
insulating them against a world that
is content to closely observe their
benighted lives without offering the
slightest bit of help, my four-dollar
beverage an extravagance, my serene
gaze a crime against their humanity

Brother/Sisters (Dysfunctional)

Did Telemachus ever waver
searching the faces of
his mother's suitors looking
for someone worthy of love?

The way we seek out strangers
to confide our various sins
while remaining distant to siblings
a remoteness often confused with hate.

Harry Lime

Color my world Payne's grey
I wither in the sunlight
Keeping to the shadows
Visible only in silhouette

Filmed in monochrome
Stripped of every hue
Bloodless like a cadaver
Elusive as the truth

Manifesto (2018)

I want to be a thorn in the lion's paw,
that itch you can't quite scratch;
A meme defeating a mechanical future,
obscene graffiti on a spotless bathroom wall.

R.I.P.

You are a finite number
your expiry date graven in stone
gone in a heartbeat
departing in a single, rattling breath

A life measured in billions of seconds
the sum simply arrived at
an equation you resist solving
to preserve some peace of mind

Hinterland Who's Who
(for Sherron)

Loving the wolf while
enduring his nips and rough play
acknowledging his territoriality
a border of piss-splattered rocks

And Sherron replies:

Loving the wolf is easy/
There is no other way to get close to the moon

Expulsion

we were never meant to be gardeners
our ambitions of a higher order
chaffing under instruction
vulnerable to sedition

Malthusian

some intimation
nameless dread
seventh sense
faculty you didn't know
shouting "Apocalypse!"
in a crowded room

American Breakdown

Alas, the pills no longer
touch the anxiety or
salve the pain

Opiates for the masses
proven ineffective
when it comes to a
soul ache originating
from frustrated desires,
thwarted dreams

Your therapist suppresses
a yawn, doodling in a
notebook, brows furrowed,
simulating concern

Not a Sonnet

Love poetry is written by
people who yearn, but can't have
the ideal they seek
that perfect Other
who might be completely oblivious
yet remains an article of faith
as real as any invisible god.

Revelation 20:19

God told me to tell you you're wrong,
your interpretations facile and outdated.

He has grown, *evolved* with the cosmos,
embarrassed by his youthful excesses.

Troubled Childhood

A history of violence
that can't be escaped

No cage strong enough to hold that beast
the jungle never far from its thoughts

A Game of Scrub

A blade off an old discer for home plate
second base always lost in the weeds
those lazy, endless July days
when we were young and wild.

In keeping with our arrogance
we believed it would last forever
never seeing the future
until it was too late to turn back.

Quantum Entanglement

You can die of thirst in open water
drown in a desert full of sand

Like two ghosts, noiselessly dancing
we leave no impression at all

Bosporus,
neither East nor West

And how "fearful" possesses
two very different connotations

The blandishments of illusion
the brittle bedrock of faith

Grasping at certainty
in a handful of air

Staunch Newtonian

substance
nothing ethereal
I need hard evidence
provable, reproducible
a diamond to masticate
between theoretical teeth

Wound

The wound speaks its own truth
giving little consideration to thoughts
of forgiveness and reconciliation

We must stop this bleeding
We must stop this bleeding
We must stop this bleeding
Before it's too late

The wound is stubborn, intractable
rejecting bandaid solutions
the comfort of a tourniquet

Sutures will never hold
relentless pressure
bursting at the seams

We must stop this bleeding
We must stop this bleeding
We must stop this bleeding
Before it's too late

The wound won't heal with time
it finds such thoughts fatuous
an affront to what it's endured

A pain so intense it distorts
each received perception
coloring them with shame

We must stop this bleeding
We must stop this bleeding
We must stop this bleeding
Before it's too late

Definition

"serendipity"
the word for when
the entire universe aligns
throwing a morsel
to some poor undeserving sod
without the accompanying usury
of shame or fault
a happy coincidence
brush with the miraculous
disguised as pure chance

Definition 2

"insular"
that quality of solitude
whereby the real world
loses all significance
reduced to a mere blur
as our inward gaze divines
the place true monsters dwell

Definition 3

"numinous"
mysterium tremendum
realm of pure spirit
occupying the space between us
transcendental
if not miraculous
strange synergies often
mistaken for ghosts

Definition 4

"despair"
a state of mind
best exemplified by
a fervent desire
to ignore the
blandishments of hope
while drawing comfort
from the certainty
that things can
always get worse

Definition 5

"melancholy"
because there is a
finite limit to happiness
and no one can safely
navigate the treacherous
shoals of perfect faith

Definition 6

"hereditary"
sense of belonging
shared traits
genetic predisposition
a familiar twisted helix
some insist is the
equivalent of Fate

Definition 7

"nihilism"
an understandable reaction
when an immature species
confuses the absence of God
with willful neglect

Definition 8

"home"
the place we feel safest
a sanctuary stone
womb we retreat to
when reality encroaches
with bared teeth
reeking of offal
starved for attention

Definition 9

"inexorable"
because Time waits for no one
a harsh regime of hours
breaking down body and spirit
so that in the end we seek only respite
quietus for our poor bones

Definition 10

"nirvana"
something resembling paradise
without the attendant guilt;
the selflessness of a bodhisattva
the blamelessness of a rose

Definition 11

"immanence"
where the spirit dwells
intangible but never aloof
sourceless and pervasive
inhabiting the smallest particle
conscious as a shining star

Definition 12

"liminal"
the space between
where stories grow
here there be monsters
submerged and waiting
caught in the act of transformation
hybrids of you and I

Definition 13

"pandemic"
a virulent acknowledgement
of our species' intrinsic desire
to destroy ourselves before
vaunting ambition compels
the stars to surrender their secrets
the technologies of Creation

We know we would make terrible gods
too enthralled with our own image
oblivious so we don't have to care

Tipping Point

At first subliminal, as in
barely noticeable, just the
slightest hint something
might be wrong

Sea changes too subtle to
detect until they engulf you,
a relentless, creeping tide

So insistent we never saw it
coming, until we did and by then
the tipping point was reached

Feigning confusion,
evincing innocence, acting
like it would never end

Nobody expects Armageddon
before the final trumpet sounds
the missiles already on their way

Hope is revealed as a
befuddlement of the
senses no longer possible
to sustain

While the future stinks
of carrion, dead things
left out in the sun

Bewhiskered

I have a rude beard/
it burns where it kisses/
creating a desire so strong/
you cannot resist/
a hirsute passion that/
scorches pliant flesh

Comfort Reading

I'm the dog-eared volume
you've read so often
the spine is broken

highlighted passages
notes scrawled in the margins
identifying your favorite parts

someday you'll finish it
but for now you tarry
reluctant to spoil the ending

Motherlove
(for Sherron)

I

the children grown
nest empty
but that kind of love
never diminishes or subsides

in truth, you worry more
than you ever did when they were
close enough to be clasped in
safe arms, preserved from harm

mothers make no accommodation
to the rapid passage of years
their all-encompassing love
refuting the predations of Time

II

We stopped counting at two
that was sufficient
a sacred number
the sum of our parts

infinity starts at nought
but has no limits
like a mother's love
it cannot be confined

Evil, Inc.

God of Hitler, Stalin, Mao
God of wasps and stinging insects
God of hurricanes, tsunamis
God of childhood cancers

Which one do *you* worship every Sunday morning
what convolutions of faith are required
to accommodate the evil loosed
at the moment of Creation?

September 19, 2020

I begged you to linger
because you kept the chill at bay
but you insisted you had
business elsewhere
and took leave of me
with an air kiss
that brushed my cheek
with the last warm breath
I'd feel until Easter
paid its ritual visit
on bended pagan knees

Some Say It Will End In Fire

A sky stained yellow/orange
the sun a distant gleam
swaddled, nearly extinguished
and, by the way, why aren't you here
sharing the apocalypse
embracing on the front step
two doomed lovers
bravely confronting their fate
slowly smothering
from secondhand smoke
an entire boreal forest
spontaneously combusting
only the latest freak of nature
forecasters reeking of entrails
promising worse to come.

Christmas, 2020

Well, we finally made it
got through the year
a very strange year
some might say *annus horribilis*
everything out of sorts

But we persevered, didn't we
once we figured out
we couldn't cling to old habits
embraced change as if we had no choice
(and we didn't)

Seek consolation in the knowledge
that things will improve, eventually,
the glimmer of hope we keep waiting for
limning the far horizon
if you know where to look

Until then, you're not alone, no, really
you mustn't think that way
critically important to understand
your isolation but a trick of the mind
this mask but a thin layer between us

An Intimation of True Genius

Before I sit down and write my masterpiece
I think I'll take a few minutes and go over my notes
check my sources and of course compose a brief
biography of the author who despite his apparent
lack of credentials has achieved true greatness with
his soon-to-be completed debut novel a sensation on
all seven continents endorsed by the glitterati honors and
prizes pouring in optioned by Hollywood dining with
royalty hobnobbing alongside jetsetters existing in
a social whirlwind object of adoration and naked envy
topping every bestseller list appearing on all the right
programs lionized by my peers no limit to my reach and
power once I *finally* find the time to buy pen and paper
take a seat at my humble desk and commence work on what
will undoubtedly become a pillar of the Western canon
my much-anticipated long-awaited magnum opus
the only story left untold

Seen

that last golden light
presaging the onset of dusk
lingering in the treetops
slowly extinguished
by suffocating night

The Double

You're someone else when you wake
a person your dream self can't recall
except for a befuddlement of images
nightmares of tedium and routine.

The Ascent of Humankind
(With apologies to Mr. Bronowski)

Life: an impulse,
resilient and infinitely adaptable

that flicker of cognition
signifying sentience

from then, it's only a
matter of time:

tool-making skills for the clever ones
religion to keep them humble

S.B.

picturing Stan Brakhage
scratching film emulsion
with his fingernails

shooting a few frames
of his dying hand shaky
16mm camera clutched in
his *other* dying hand

the devotion & strength of mind
it would take

an impulse to create
in defiance of extinction
artist to his last breath

Science Fiction

envisioning tomorrow
the ultimate "what if"

who can fathom the
inexplicable intentions
of Providence

or (conversely) extrapolate
what an accidental universe
might manifest exalt
or condemn

Space Telescope

the tallest spire cannot hope to achieve
a perspective so vast it encompasses
even a tiny portion of infinity

that magnitude of galaxies
a mere handful of Creation

Stages

Sorrow: a bottomless pit

Grief: acknowledging a terrible absence

Time: new skin on exposed flesh

Courage: in the face of loneliness

Despair: when it becomes too much

Faith: a call answered

Fanatic

I've suspended my disbelief
eager to apprehend
a vision of Creation
that doesn't require me to think

Faith moves mountains
makes the blind see
no further proofs required
when doubt is tantamount to heresy

Estrangement

you have become estranged from me
a neighborhood of broken windows
discouraging any visitor
from lingering there

your wooden kisses
leave little splinters
your contempt a weapon
wielded by expert hands

    the walls are cracking
    ceiling coming down
    like Samson in the temple we are
    self-killed by the weight of stones

Pagans

once a year
we don elaborate costumes
terrorizing the community with silly antics

we enjoy playing monsters
symbolically devouring our neighbors
down to their wide-eyed children

"Shhhh…"

Libraries aren't silent any more
the pings of cell phones
not shushed by attentive librarians
and no one rouses the bums
polluting the air space of the magazine
section, or frowns at the small child
having a meltdown at the checkout
counter, which in five years will
be fully automated and even more
immune to the fuss

The Beginning of Wisdom

Let us not speak of certainties
(they make a mockery of reason)
and instead sing praises to doubt
(one of the building blocks of faith).

Come, No Man,
perfect in every way;
we are made in the image of God
flawed, yet wise enough to know shame.

Weightless

I miss the resistance of air
but not the weight of gravity

the stars so much brighter here
in such close proximity to heaven

Almanac

I regret to inform you the lilies are dying
also those ferns you like by the garage
the zinnias petrifying on their long stems
even our stalwart Maltese Crosses
wilted and sclerotic

The best part of summer is gone
the sun receding in the sky—
soon another season will arrive
brightly attired but cool
to the touch

Uninhibited

I am your today your tomorrow
all your yesterdays
combined

it's not a matter of Delphic wisdom
more a case of knowing exactly
where to put my fingers

your songs of love and laughter
all the compensation I require
for services rendered

in our secret rooms
removed from their scrutiny
impervious to shame

uninhibited
(the way we
use our mouths)

Renegades

We'll go on committing our love crimes
in defiance of accepted norms
openly embracing to the disgust of neighbors
weeping when we part

The Quality of Mercy

Mercy
must be as undiscriminating
as a new mother gazing in
awe at the child nuzzling her breast.

There can be no conditions or exceptions
or caveats since, after all, we have,
every one of us, sinned against God,
Nature and Love.

Sobriety Test

can you read this page
does it make sense
find your cock
now get it to work
name your children
their birthdays
social insurance number
count by threes to a hundred
walk a straight line
don't hide bottles
or slur your words
get drunk on life
avoiding the inevitable hangovers
lose the anxiety and soul dread
without chemical assistance
take back control
before it's too late

Night Sweats

stop your weeping
your spendthrift heart still
mistakes the slightest hurt
for a cataclysm too
horrific to be endured

when will you learn
the worst cannot be
imagined any more than
you can anticipate a bolt
of lightning on a clear day

bad news is clever
waiting 'til you're
not looking then
pretending to come
upon you by chance

This Place

we're here
there are no roads back
the future written
now it must be endured

Epistemology

and you didn't linger over roses
marking their conscious perfection

instead you saw chaos
and drew the obvious conclusion

but the miraculous is every day present
too tangible to be denied

god, all-pervasive
the devil in the details

Arahant

I have achieved
a whole other level
of insane

losing all coherence
invisibly moving
among you

piercing the veil
so the Light can
get through

the received Logos
and the inevitable
unbinding

from a tall promontory
for the best view of
what comes next

Yule

Be the star
at the top of the tree
drape yourself in lights
to depose December's gloom;

how many gifts can you give
to satisfy the generosity
of your swelling heart
without spending a dime;

never failing to leave cookies
for the Spirit of the season
those inexplicable dusty footprints
stamped in the chimney hearth.

Lost

ambiguity: the point
where all roads end

slowturning
thunderous heartthrobs

seeking familiarity
something unnatural

too ugly to be placed there
by chance

Moonglow
(for Sherron)

I told the moon
what I'd done
and how I wished to atone

she said it wasn't within her purview
to confer absolution
denying my humble suit

instead she bade me ply the stars
so distant and so deaf—
but not to expect forbearance
in the cold, deep and dark

Noisy Ghost

    I swear I hear you in the house
sometimes even though I'm fully
aware you're hundreds of miles away
visiting the grandkids.

    It could only be you
making the hardwood creak
outside the bedroom door
the invisible presence
pushing past me on the stairs.

    It's like some part of you
remained here determined
to watch over me keep me
out of mischief knowing I
tend to lapse into melancholy
when you're not around.

Cliff Burns has been an independent author and publisher for more than thirty years. He has written sixteen full-length books, as well as penning numerous radio and stage plays, reviews and commentaries. His poems and short stories have appeared in well over a hundred publications and anthologies around the world. He lives in western Canada with his wife, artist and educator Sherron Harman Burns.

www.ingramcontent.com/pod-product-compliance
Lightning Source LLC
Chambersburg PA
CBHW031003090426
42737CB00008B/651